Important to ~~others.~~
me.

Quotes I love

Made me feel
something

Also by Jasmine Cepeda:

*12 Ways to Cope With Your
Latino Dad & His Difficulties*

12 Ways to Cope With

Your Latina Mom & Her Difficulties

a guided journal

3rd Edition

by Jasmine Cepeda, LCSW
Illustrations by Albie Bernabel

betternowtherapy.org

Independently Published
Brooklyn, New York

Disclaimer

The information provided in this book is designed to provide helpful information on the topics discussed. This book is not meant to be used, nor should it be used to diagnose or treat any mental health condition. For therapy treatment of any, consult your physician or therapist.

The author is not responsible for any specific mental health issues that may require clinical treatment and is not liable for any damages or negative consequences of any action, application, treatment to any person reading this book.
Content is not a substitute for therapy/replacement for formal therapy

ISBN: 9781704366791

Illustrations by Albie Bernabel
Al.bernabel80@gmail.com

Book Design by Jasmine Cepeda
Fonts Used:
Book Title: Homemade Apple Designed by Font Diner
https://fonts.google.com/specimen/Homemade+Apple
Content: Muli Normal by Vernon Adams
https://fonts.google.com/specimen/Muli
Chapter Titles: Chelsea Market by Paul D. Hunt
https://fonts.google.com/specimen/Chelsea+Market

Visit us on the web!
www.betternowtherapy.org

Tag Us!
#latinamomsbook
@betternowtherapy

Dedicated to:

my Latinx clients, the
Latinx community,
and all Latina/x
Mothers!

12 Ways to Cope With
Your Latina Mom
& Her Difficulties

Table of Contents

PART 2: RE-MOTHERING &
SELF-PROTECTION

Introduction

As a Psychotherapist raised and still living in the diverse mega-city that is NYC, I have helped hundreds of folks from all races, ethnicities, and cultures cope with their distressing feelings and thoughts about their mothers.

However, what makes me especially inclined to write about the nuanced difficulties of Latina mothers is my experience in facilitating groups with Latinx individuals (a gender-neutral term for Latinas and Latinos) struggling with their mothers. Being involved in these groups has clarified the similar and overarching grievances that many Latinx folks experience.

Moreover, rather than writing for all people, women, or women of color, I am writing for the Latinx community as a Latinx. All people can have difficulties with their mothers. Yet, there are some things that Latina moms do and say that are very specific to being Latinx—whether it's the words they choose to guilt-trip you with or the prayers they recite when you fall from their graces, having a Latina mom has its unique attributes.

Although I accept that the "Latinx" label is also broad and includes various races, nationalities, countries, and cultures, I find that the identity has its worth and validity as a shared identity, one that should be acknowledged and affirmed.

The shared language (mainly Spanish), culture (foods, religion, rituals, etc.), and history of the Latinx community in the United States are genuine commonalities. On that note, I acknowledge the layer of difference involving

Latinx folks who are not born, raised, or live in the U.S. I did write this guide from the perspective of a Latinx born and raised in the U.S, in an immigrant household, and most of my Latinx clients who were part of my groups have similar characteristics.

Yet, I still believe that many Latinx individuals outside of the U.S. can relate to the topics in this guide. Although the oxford dictionary states that "Latinx" emerged in the early 21st century as an "American Spanish" word, the internet has helped the label transcend boundaries.

Unfortunately, this book is mainly in English, but I hope to translate it into Spanish one day!

Regarding the title of this project: I do not want to promote a false narrative that Latina moms are inherently "difficult" or all the same. Many Latina moms have nurturing and deep emotional relationships with their children and do not constantly behave in challenging ways. Hence, I describe the behaviors as "difficult," not who they are.

Also, the label "mother" in this guide represents whomever you consider "mother," whether it's your biological mother, grandmother, aunt, or a maternal figure.

Moreover, this guide is best for folks >18. "Child" in this guide indicates that the person is the mother's child, not that I am solely speaking about children.

Reference: "Latinx." Lexico Dictionaries Powered by Oxford. Oxford University Press. https://www.lexico.com/en/definition/latinx.

"Latinx:" A Label That's Trying

"Latinx" is a gender-neutral term for "Latina" or "Latino." It is helpful for folks who identify as queer or non-conforming genders. But even if you are of Latin-American descent and identify as cisgender (i.e., identify with the sex assigned at birth), you can still identify as "Latinx." For instance, you can identify as both "Latino" and "Latinx." Identifying with "Latinx" does not erase your identity as a cisgender man, likewise for cis-gendered women or Latinas.

You do not have to identify as "queer" or "non-conforming" to identity as "Latinx," which highlights why the "Latinx" label is not just about gender. Identifying as "Latinx" is also about saying NO to the gendered stereotypes and pressures that exist in the Latin American community. It is a way to show solidarity, as well as stand up for yourself.

Meditating on the word "Latinx," I thought about why I describe the mothers of Latinx folks as "Latinas" and not "Latinx." Unconsciously, or without really thinking about it, I labeled the mothers as "Latinas" because—to describe them as "Latinx" would connect them to a generation, a movement, and a label that they may not understand or use themselves. Yes, this is an assumption, just in the same way I am assuming that "Latinx" is the new, accepted term that all millennials or younger folks of Latin-American decent use. But I am sure not all young folks identify as "Latinx," yet, I am using it to describe them, so is this guide for them?

Yes, it still is. This guide is for all folks who identify as "Latinx," "Latina," "Latino," "Hispanic," or "Spanish," which is a label I grew up hearing (and still here) in NYC.

"Latinx" appears to be a term implying "wokeness" and attempting to be inclusive and progressive, even though it is too broad and one word can never describe so many people.

Still, as stated before, "Latinx" is a valid and crucial identity. It came to fruition based on necessity, reflecting the reality of our times and the desire to push our culture to be more inclusive. The "Latinx" identity represents both the collective and the individual. It is beautiful in its attempt and usage. It's trying.

· · · · · · · · · · · · · · · · · · · ·

Journal

1. How do you identify? "Latina/o," "Hispanic," "Spanish," "Latinx?" Why?

Intentions for this Guide

I intend to help you explore the psychological consequences of having a mother with difficult behaviors. I will guide you in setting boundaries and acting towards self-validation and self-protection. I also want to help you remother (or reparent) yourself and your inner child—to help you build your self-compassion. By building a better relationship with yourself, I want to assist you in creating better relationships with others: whether it's with your mother, friends, romantic partner, or as a parent! Lastly, I will guide you in exploring the burden and gift of ending your family's intergenerational trauma through the practices in this book.

As you go through this guide, know that you can stay in each step (or feeling states [like anger or sadness]) as long as you'd like—there is no need to rush your process! Healing takes time and is not linear. There may be times you regress or need to pause. It is all okay.

Another vital aspect of this guide is journaling (having a second blank journal may help, if you find yourself needing more space to write).

I will usually ask you about three separate parts of your conscious psyche:
1. **your feelings** (emotional states that can be uncomfortable but necessary to experience)
2. **your cognition/thoughts** (which may be valid and accurate interpretations or assumptions that lack evidence)
3. **your behaviors/actions** (Feelings and thoughts motivate our behaviors. Thus, it can be helpful to take a step back [before acting] and focus on your internal happening).

Our feelings, thoughts, and actions are conscious (in our awareness). It is hard for us to delve into our *unconscious* (what is out of our awareness) without someone to reflect with—which is why psychotherapy is beneficial.

I encourage you to start (or continue) therapy during this journey, where you may explore your unconscious. I recommend you inform yourself of your therapist's modality to ensure the best fit. Some therapists focus on uncovering the unconscious, while others focus on conscious awareness.

In the meantime, I recommend Aldo Pucci's, *The Client's Guide to Cognitive-Behavioral Therapy*, which can help you reflect on your conscious thoughts and feelings.

Journal

1. Why did you pick up this guide?

I picked this guide to help me start journaling.

2. How do you feel about your answer above?

I feel powerful.

3. What feelings do you want to have by the end of this book? Why?

I want to be okay.

Una Nota Para Las Madres Que Leen Esta Guía

If you are a mother reading this thinking that you are "difficult" or engage in difficult behaviors towards your children, know that *this guide is also for you!* This guide highlights why it is unhealthy to depend on your children to meet your emotional needs and the psychological consequences for both parties.

I also encourage you to go to therapy or begin the path towards self-exploration and healing; ultimately, taking responsibility for meeting your own needs. Doing your work in self-actualization will help you have a healthier bond with your children.

Again, this book is also for you—to heal yourself, your relationship with your children, and possibly your relationship with your own mother.

A Note About Your Dad

I could have titled this guide "Your Latinx Parents and Their Difficulties," but I believe that would have minimized the harmful effects of the machismo and sexist culture that often defines being raised in a Latin-American family. That being said, your relationship with your father may not be much better than your relationship with your mother. For that reason, I also wrote 12 Ways to Cope With Your Latino Dad & His Difficulties (2021).

Even if your father was not Latino, living in a patriarchal world has probably affected all of us, including your father and how his role in the family, and your mother and how she treats you. We will further examine Gender and Sexuality later in this guide.

It is essential to take a moment to remember how your father has treated you and your mother and the many ways his treatment or difficult behaviors may have affected the family dynamics.

For example, was your dad physically absent (which made your mother a single parent), or was he emotionally unavailable, aggressive, abusive, submissive, or passive? Did they divorce? And if so, how did that affect you? Do you have step-parents/siblings? And if so, do you like them? Or is your dad in a codependent/toxic relationship with your mother? Etc.

Journal

On the next page, journal/free-write about your father and how he has affected your family dynamics.

- emotionally unavailable

- A sweet Dad

- Risked his family

- yells doesn't talks

- fixes everything

- Buys us everything

9

Ending Intergenerational Trauma

In Part 2, you will reflect on your mother's deep psychological wounds. It will help you empathize and understand her in her family context.

For now, I want to focus on the lineage of ancestors shared by you and your mother. These ancestors may have brought both joy and trauma into the family. Deciding to confront and heal generational wounds is powerful. By reading this book, reflecting, going to therapy, and "doing the work," you are already putting a dent in ending family toxic patterns.

Intergenerational trauma is a term used to describe the influence of traumatic experiences on multiple family generations. In 1966, Canadian psychiatrist Vivian M. Rakoff, MD and her colleagues highlighted the presence of psychological distress in children of Holocaust survivors (*Canada's Mental Health*, Vol. 14). It was one of the first articles shining a light on generational trauma. Since then, many researchers and therapists have studied the phenomenon and the term has gained wide-popularity among our society.

Traumas like sexual abuse, substance abuse, domestic violence, homophobia, extreme poverty, slavery, and colonialism can be deeply hidden in the family fabric, and thus, get passed on.

Four reasons why intergenerational trauma may get passed are:
1) the lack of mental health services available during the traumatic event
2) the stigma around getting treatment for mental health concerns
3) the deep denial of the trauma itself
4) and lastly, the minimization, normalization, or gaslighting about the trauma.

The dysfunctional family dynamics that have repeated over and over can end now, with you! You can start a new lineage and stop the cycle. If you continue to normalize the dysfunction, it will continue to get passed on.

Take a moment to express gratitude to your ancestors and family members who have gotten you to the position where you are right now. In this very moment, you have privileges (like time, space, education, or money) that they did not have, but they helped you attain. With these tools, you can now delve deeper into unhealthy family patterns and stop them (which they did not have the privilege of doing).

Below are some book recommendations to further explore your intergenerational trauma:
- *My Grandmother's Hands* by Resmaa Menakem
- *It Didn't Start With You* by Mark Wolynn
- *Intergenerational Trauma Workbook* by Lynne Friedman-Gell and Joanne Barron

•••••••••••••••••••••

Conscious Decision-Making to Have Kids or Not

Regardless of how your caregivers raised you, it will unquestionably affect how you raise your children (if you have children). For folks who want to be parents (or already have kids), I hope you can learn how to heal from your mother's challenging behaviors so that you can become a better parent and end unhealthy family patterns.

For those who do not know if they want kids, I also want to assist you in building a clearer sense of your own experience being "mothered" and how it may affect your decision.

For folks who are childfree by choice (or are thinking about it), I'd like to help you build

11

insight into how weak or strong your decision is tied to your relationship with your mother, primary caregiver, or family dynamics.

Some people (unconsciously or not) decide **not** to have kids because they are dissatisfied with their relationships with their parents. They grow up not valuing the parent-child relationship because their primary caregiver/s may have been emotionally neglectful, distant, or abusive.

Moreover, folks may opt-out of having a traditional family with children (and possibly create their own "chosen family" with friends) because of the many painful memories that exist around their family relationships.

What's more, some women reject and resent the maternal identity because they do not want to identify with anything related to their mothers.

I want to help you make any of your life decisions, including to have children or not, from a place of hope and power, not **scarcity**. Just because you did not have satisfying relations with your caregivers, it does not mean you cannot be a great caregiver in the future!

If you still do not want to have children after increasing your self-understanding, your decision will be more well-grounded.

Journal

1. What are your **thoughts** and **feelings** on having kids/or not?

I wand a kid Rignt

now.

Choosing the Best Partner

Unconsciously, individuals can sometimes date folks with personalities or ways of being similar to those of their parents. This occurs because their relationship dynamic with their new partner (whether healthy or not) feels familiar because it is something the individual has already experienced with their caregivers. Some folks call it "chemistry" when it is *familiarity*.

Because of this, it is vital to identify and process your feelings about your mother's difficult behaviors (and any negative messages that you have internalized from her) so that you can increase your self-worth and not fall into toxic romantic relationships.

In this guide, you will identify your unmet interpersonal needs. **Interpersonal needs** are those that you cannot fulfill by yourself and are met in relationships. Interpersonal needs include (but are not limited to): feeling a sense of belonging, care, positive attention, understanding, support, and inclusion.

It is important to let go of (what may be) **unrealistic expectations** that your mother will meet your interpersonal needs. Letting go of the fantasy will force you to try to meet your needs elsewhere. And it will help you decrease your tolerance of being with a partner who is unwilling (or incapable) of meeting your interpersonal needs.

Journal

1. Have any of your past (or current) romantic relationships mirrored the dynamic you have with your mother? If so, who and how?

Yes, my first relationship. There was the same selfish remarks.

2. What are your **thoughts** and **feelings** about this?

I don't care.

Part 1
Self-
Validation

This part of the guide involves identifying and acknowledging your feelings, thoughts, behaviors, and triggers concerning your mother's difficult behaviors. Labeling and verbalizing these things is a way to *self-validate* and increase your *self-respect*. This part aims to increase your self-awareness and decrease your self-doubt. The uncomfortable part is coming face-to-face with your many distressing feelings. The rest of the guide will help you build your tolerance and cope with these feelings.

1. Your Self-tending Routine

"Self-care" appears to have become a capitalistic trend, which is why I no longer use the term. Instead, I believe in *self-tending*. I like the word "tend" because it reminds you to attend and be tender with yourself.

Sadly, if your mother did not attend to you as a child or was rarely tender with you, it can be hard to know what it feels or looks like to self-tend.

Self-tending means paying attention and being curious about what you need at the moment. It means practicing self-compassion, gentleness, and rest. It also means taking an active role in protecting your well-being and peace of mind.

Because delving into your feelings and thoughts about your mother will be difficult, your unique and individual self-tending routine is crucial.

Whether your self-tending routine involves seeking a therapist to guide you through this journey, practicing loving-kindness meditation, or hanging out with your friends, one meaningful way to cope with your mother's difficulties is to self-tend.

My Self-Tending Routine!

List 10 ways you will self-tend. Make sure to always come back to this list like an "emergency kit" when feeling down or overwhelmed.

- Therapy
- friends
- Shopping
- Sister time
- Boyfriend
- Alone time

Music Therapy

Create an uplifting, self-tending playlist!

2. Feeling Your Feelings & Self-Soothing/Regulating

Gaining insight into how you honestly feel and think about your relationship with your mother can have moments of sadness and anger and periods of peace and relief.

Hence, coping with your mom and her difficulties means accepting your unpleasant feeling and coping with these feelings as they arise.

The first thing to know about emotions is that they are not "good" or "bad," they just are. You do not have to judge yourself for your feelings. Feelings will give you **information** about how you are genuinely experiencing something or someone.

Secondly, you are not "weak" or "dramatic" for having emotions. Letting go of these internalized messages from your family or society will help you accept your feelings. Continuing to deny or repress your feelings will only deteriorate your mental health.

Thirdly, feelings are like waves. They can be HUGE and overwhelming and feel SCARY, but huge waves (just like huge feelings) can also be spectacular and bring you ultimate relief! Or, like smaller waves, emotions can be subtle but still move you.

The following page lists common feelings, but please feel free to google even more feelings!

You can always come back to this list when exploring your feelings.

Welcome and allow all the feelings about your mother to pass through you. Just like waves or clouds, your feelings are temporary states. The release is where the healing happens.

Feelings

Acceptance	Empathetic	Remorse
Ambivalence	Frustrated	Restless
Anger	Fear	Sadness
Annoyance	Forgiving	Self-conscious
Anxiety	Hesitant	Shame
Appreciative	Hopeful	Thankful
Ashamed	Ignored	Tired
Calm	Indifferent	Uneasy
Centered	Insecure	Unfulfilled
Confident	Jealous	Uninvolved
Courageous	Joyful	Unsafe
Curious	Loving	Unstable
Disappointed	Open	Unsure
Disconnected	Overwhelmed	Weary
Discouraged	Powerful	Withdrawn
Disgust	Powerless	Worried
Doubtful	Perplexed	Yearning

Emotion Regulation/Self-Soothing Strategies

We are not born with emotional regulation skills. These skills need to be taught or modeled to us as children. It might be hard to feel or regulate your emotions (or self-soothe) if you grew up with a caregiver or mother who

1. did not control or regulate their own emotions
2. did not help soothe you when you were upset
3. did not make it safe for your feelings to be expressed
4. did not validate your emotions
5. and did not teach you how to regulate or cope with your emotions.

If no one taught you how to cope with your feelings or did not allow for a safe space to do so, you might have built defense mechanisms against unpleasant feelings. For example, you may have **repressed** your emotions or expressed them **uncontrollably** or impulsively (i.e., throwing things, hitting, lashing out, or hurting yourself).

Sometimes folks dramatically express their feelings because they believe others do not take their feelings seriously enough or respond adequately. This does not invalidate their feelings—it merely shows one's desire to be seen and heard. Still, uncontrollably expressing your feelings can make it hard to communicate effectively and may push people away.

For example, many of the problematic behaviors that your mother engages in might push you away. What's more, she may behave in these ways because she has had a history of not being taken seriously or being emotionally validated. Still, her poor emotional regulation skills are not your responsibility to fix. But you can repair your self-soothing abilities.

Calming the body and breath is the first vital step to emotional self-regulation. In order to name your feelings, think rationally, and communicate effectively, it is crucial to control your **physiological responses** (or your body's "fight-flight-freeze-faint" reaction) to distressing thoughts or emotions.

When feeling anxious or fearful, it is normal for your body to respond with increased heart rate, sweaty hands, blushing, etc. What is most important is recognizing your body's response and trying to calm these responses down so that you can process reality.

Using your five senses to ground yourself is enormously helpful (i.e., drinking cold water, touching something smooth, imagining something calming, hearing a song or sound you like, or smelling lavender or an aroma you enjoy).

Mindfulness meditation and grounding techniques are extremely helpful in bringing you back to your five senses and slowing down the breath with diaphragmatic breathing. If you feel you have severe anxiety, I highly recommend talking to a therapist or doctor, along with the numerous books on using mindfulness strategies to reduce anxiety.

Then, *labeling* your emotions is the second part of self-regulation. To help you build awareness of your feelings, it may helpful to track how you are specifically feeling each day. I recommend using one of the many "mood-tracking" apps that currently exist.

Journal

1. Growing up, how did your mother control or regulate her emotions?

2. How did your mother try to soothe you (if she did try) when you were upset as a child?

3. If she did not help soothe you, how did you soothe yourself? Did you pick up her habits regarding how she controlled and regulated her emotions?

4. Has your mother gotten better with regulating her emotions or being emotionally supportive towards you?

Journal

1. When you think about your mother, what feelings arise automatically? (examples: happiness, love, anger, resentment, etc.)
(TIP: identify the precise feelings using the list of feelings)

2. What memories (if any) are attached to these feelings?

3. Identity 1-3 pleasant feelings about your mother, along with associated memories. Find a photo of you and your mom that reminds you of these feelings. Look at the photo and reflect.

4. Identity 1-3 unpleasant feelings about your mother, along with associated memories.

3. Accepting Ambivalence: Letting Go of the "She's All Bad" Narrative

No mother (or person) is perfect. No mother is "all good" or "all bad." As the last exercise illustrates, there can be both pleasant and unpleasant thoughts, feelings, and memories associated with your mother. She is not all "bad." On the contrary, the positive feelings and memories only show you the potential to enjoy her company.

It is vital to give yourself space to be in the gray and not in extreme black or white (all or nothing, polarized) states of mind. **Ambivalence** (or having mixed/contradictory ideas/ feelings about something or someone) is a feeling that some folks avoid because it does not lend itself to certainty or control. However, we cannot always have certainty or control. Most things are not perfect and fall in the gray area. *Building your tolerance for uncertainty and ambivalence will help you tremendously in your healing process.*

By letting go of the narrative that she is "all bad," you are letting go of that version of yourself that needs *her to "stay bad." This version of yourself wants to* stay resentful, hurt, sad, etc. *By letting go of that narrow storyline, you are making more* r o o m *and space for other feelings (like forgiveness, empathy, gratitude, and love/care towards your mother). Releasing your reliance on the "she's all bad" narrative changes your identity, especially if you have lost yourself in the binary storyline.*

Letting go of the "she's all bad" narrative does not mean falling into the "she's all good/it's all good" narrative. Accepting your ambivalence means accepting that you have mixed feelings about her, not that you eliminate or excuse her negative behavior.

At times, you may have more distressing feelings, thoughts, and memories about your mother than positive ones. This is, of course, valid, especially if she has engaged in more difficult behaviors than healthy ones.

•••••••••••••••••••••

Journal

1. Do you often think in "black or white" or "all or nothing" terms? Explain.

2. Do you feel that you have trouble with feeling uncertainty or lack of control?

3. What would it be like to accept your ambivalent feelings about your mother?

4. Though it may be uncomfortable, can you accept being "in the gray?"

5. If you have a narrative that your mother is "all bad," what would it look like for you to let go of that storyline?

6. Do you feel that you have lost your identity in binary storylines?

Being Clear on Her Level of Difficulty

Society seems to accept that parents, especially moms, can be "difficult." It is normal to have grievances about your mother and to share them with others openly.

However, to help differentiate between difficult behaviors that are psychologically detrimental from those that are less so, I have created the "Behaviors and Their Level of Difficulty Spectrum." I created the spectrum from my extensive experience as a psychotherapist, not from scientific research. The **"Behaviors and Their Level of Difficulty Spectrum"** is a conceptual/illustrative model that can be applied to any individual in your life (not just mothers), including yourself. This model has helped me understand my clients and may help you too!

I did not focus on the difficult behaviors themselves to create this spectrum because I have found that it can be culturally insensitive and unhelpful to try to generalize what is or isn't "difficult" behavior. I do not believe any behavior is inherently "difficult," I think that the level of "difficulty" is on a continuum. The following criteria describe how behaviors are established as mildly to extremely difficult.

"Behaviors and Their Level of Difficulty Spectrum"
By Jasmine Cepeda, LCSW

Mildly   Moderately   Severely   Extremely

The criteria I use to define a difficult behavior is:
1. how it makes the person on the receiving end feel**
2. how aware the perpetrator is of the behavior/s being problematic
3. how willing the perpetrator is to try to understand the sufferer's perspective
4. and how willing the perpetrator is to change and take accountability.

For example, a mother can guilt-trip their child about coming home for thanksgiving and make their child feel angry and misunderstood. The guilt-tripping can be seen as a "difficult behavior." However, after the child communicates to their mother about how important "friendsgiving" will be this year, the mother may become understanding, flexible, and apologize. Because the mother is supportive, the "level of difficulty" is "mild," compared to a mother who continues her "severe" manipulation.

As you can see, what makes a difficult behavior troubling is the person is unwilling to acknowledge your pain, take accountability, and change after you communicate your unpleasant feelings about the behavior. We will shortly explore effective communication, which is necessary for a healthy relationship.

**Your feelings must be based on reality. Your feelings cannot be disproportionate or exaggerated to the event (though what is "disproportionate" or "exaggerated" feelings can be subjective). If you feel you do not have a good judgment or handle on your feelings, or that you feel emotions "intensely," or find them "overwhelming," it may be hard to ascertain if your feelings are "proportionate" to the event. It might be helpful to seek help from a therapist or professional.

On one end of the spectrum, we have "mildly" difficult, which most of us have experienced. These behaviors usually make us feel annoyed, but it seems to be a form of "maternal instinct," which is why it can be troublesome for moms to stop. Here are some examples: your mother telling you to clean up after yourself, lecturing you about your social status and preferences, or oversharing to others about your successes or failures (in a positive way). These behaviors do not usually hurt our self-esteem or self-worth or jeopardize our relationship with our mothers. Still, they are very annoying.

"Behaviors and Their Level of Difficulty Spectrum"
By Jasmine Cepeda, LCSW

| Mildly | Moderately | Severely | Extremely |

Next on the spectrum is "moderately" difficult. These behaviors lead us to feel low self-esteem, insecure, and unworthy (as well as annoyed). However, our mothers are aware of these behaviors bothering us and are open to changing or stopping them. Examples of these behaviors can be: bullying, commenting on your weight, criticizing what you're wearing, comparing you to others, etc., criticizing (not just lecturing) you about your social status and preferences.

These behaviors may underlie a desire for mothers to control their children through being harsh.

However, once their child communicates their pain, moms who practice these "moderately" difficult behaviors feel guilty and try their hardest to stop (and usually do).

Some behaviors are so obviously hurtful that the mother can apologize and stop on her own (without their child communicating how hurt they feel). This also shows the child that their mother is attending to her child's needs for attunement and emotional support, which we will later examine in this guide.

Following on the spectrum is "severely" difficult. These behaviors lead us to feel self-doubt and low self-worth (as well as low self-esteem, insecurity, unworthy, and annoyance). Moms who practice these problematic behaviors are open to understanding how they make you feel and also feel guilty.

These mothers can have a tough time stopping these difficult behaviors because the behaviors are a way to release their unpleasant feelings (such as depression, anxiety, anger, etc.), and calm down from them—sometimes *displacing* or *projecting* their emotions onto their child. This *displacement* or *projection* may lead the child to *internalize* their mother's negative feelings or make the child feel they are to blame for the negative emotions. Or even worse, it may make the child believe that the verbal attacks from their mother are valid and acceptable.

Essentially, the difficult behaviors at this level tend to be tied to your mother's *poor coping strategies for her distressing feelings*. Change in your mother depends on **her** ability to practice healthier coping strategies to identify, express, and accept her feelings. We will explore how **you** can change in Part 2.

Because the "severe" behaviors are more abrasive or cruel, this level is like "turning the degrees up" from the "moderately" difficult behaviors. Examples of severe behaviors include: verbally attacking you with harsh names or words or harshly criticizing your decision-making and lifestyle. These moms may have an unhealthy habit of using their children as punching bags for their unpleasant feelings. And similar to the last level, their actions may stem from a desire to control.

Because it is a spectrum, your mother may lie in between levels, which is understandable since human beings are dynamic and not static.

Lastly, we have "extremely" difficult behaviors. These behaviors may lead us to feel powerless, guilt, and shame. They can also increase our self-doubt (as well as decrease our self-worth, self-esteem, security, etc.) In these states, mothers may not be very open in trying to stop these behaviors. These difficult behaviors are usually **manipulative**, exploitative, discrediting, self-centered, and harsh. Some examples include: twisting your words around, demanding you listen to them, minimizing your thoughts and feelings, shaming you, minimizing your success, highlighting your failures, blaming you for their harsh behavior, denying they did anything wrong, not apologizing, appearing envious or jealous of you, or competing with you. Nothing is ever good enough for these mothers.

The mothers in this state are in denial and want to maintain **power** in the relationship.

What's more, some mothers may not be as psychologically capable or strong enough to stop their difficult behaviors because they have a **mental health disorder**.

Many of the difficult behaviors stem from emotional immaturity or poor emotional self-regulation skills.

Severely and Extremely Difficult Behaviors Are Abusive & Traumatizing

Abuse is traumatizing and comes in many forms—verbal, financial, physical, psychological, sexual, etc. Severely and extremely difficult behaviors can be abusive, but only you get to say if you are in an abusive relationship or not. It does not matter if others may think you are in an abusive relationship because you do not. You may or may not be in denial, but either way, you are not ready to label it as "abuse." 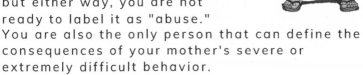 You are also the only person that can define the consequences of your mother's severe or extremely difficult behavior.

If you feel your mother is abusive or toxic, and the chances of her changing are low, it is your right to protect yourself in any way possible. You do not have to tolerate abuse! We will explore setting boundaries in Part 2.

Having a narcissistic mother can be traumatizing as well—since she may warp reality. When you are doing what she wants, she may praise you and put you on a high pedestal since she thinks of you as an extension of herself. But when you don't do what she wants, you may fall very low, and she may say horrible things to you or act in extreme or impulsive ways. You have the right to protect yourself from such hazardous behaviors.

Unfortunately, some folks may unconsciously internalize their mother's selfishness or "black or white" thinking.

If Your Mother Has a Mental Health Dx

Not all mental health issues need a diagnosis. The Diagnostic and Statistical Manual of Mental Disorders, 5th ed. (DSM–5), is written by the American Psychiatric Association and is the most widely used manual for therapists to classify and diagnose mental disorders. Though the DSM (and the field of psychology) has had a long history of being racist, sexist, and homophobic, mental health disorders do exist. Still, as a feminist, I denounce the over-pathologizing and over-diagnosing of women's mental health, especially BIPOC women.

If your mother does indeed have a mental health disorder, it may be helpful to skim the DSM-5 and educate yourself on her disorder. This may help you **understand** her actions and help you **empathize** with your mother.

Having any mental health issue may cause your mother to have a poor sense of reality. She may live in irrational, delusional, depressive, anxious, or narcissistic states of mind. However, you are not responsible for taking care of her mental health. She is the only person that must take steps to be seen by a professional.

Regardless if your mother has been officially diagnosed or not, what matters is not always the diagnosis but how she makes you feel. Does she make you feel ignored (may be caused by depression), or restless (may be caused by anxiety), or worried (may be caused by a manic episode), or unworthy (may be caused by narcissistic personality disorder). Whatever the professional diagnosis, trouble with coping with your unpleasant feelings about your mother is why you are reading this guide. Your mental health matters too! It would be best if you focused on your mental health.

Emotionally Neglectful or Emotionally Unavailable Behaviors

Emotionally neglectful (or unavailable, inaccessible, distant, disengaged) behaviors can also be challenging to handle and have serious, long-lasting effects. In the most severe cases, it may lie in between "Severe" and "Extreme" on the "Behaviors and Their Level of Difficulty" spectrum.

It is unrealistic to think moms can be "on" 24/7 when many stressors are on their minds. However, mothers need to be "on" more often than not because that is what the child will remember the most. We will soon explore the severe consequences of failing to be emotionally available for your children.

Sadly some mothers may also suffer from mental health disorders such as depression, bipolar, or substance abuse, which may cause their emotional distance.

Children (and adult children) may unconsciously interpret their mothers' emotional disengagement in unhealthy ways that may cause low self-esteem, low self-worth, little self-interest, and even depression. They may have thoughts like, "She doesn't care," "She's disinterested," "I'm not interesting enough," "I'm not enough," etc. It is natural and logical to see why children may take their mother's behavior personally since they do not know what may be truly going on.

Often, it can be helpful for parents with severe mental health disorders to find a therapist for their child, where they may gain social and emotional support in the midst of their parent having an episode, or being inconsistent with 37 their attention.

Kids may also begin to become upset and "act out" because they may sense (or internalize messages) that they have been "forgotten." Therapy can also help children in this stage.

•••••••••••••••••••

Journal

1. Growing up, what emotionally distant or disengaged behaviors did your mother show?

2. What are your thoughts about this?

3. Have you internalized negative self-talk about your mother's distance/ disengagement? What are the negative statements?

4. Did you go to therapy as a child? If so, why? If not, do you think it may have helped?

5. Does she continue these distant/disengaged behaviors into your adulthood? If so, what are your thoughts and feelings about this?

#4 Practicing Effective Communication & Self-Respect

Part of deciphering the severity of your mother's behaviors means giving her the chance to change. For her to change, you need to communicate your feelings and thoughts. Hence, we will explore some tools for effective communication.

Increasing your ability to communicate with your mother will help you express your feelings, thoughts, and needs. Communication is also the first step in establishing your boundaries (further explored in Part 2). If you have trouble communicating with your mother because of language barriers, we will also touch on that obstacle (pg 53).

There are many methods for effective communication. Below are some books on particular styles.

- *Say What You Mean* by Oren Jay Sofer
- *Nonviolent Communication: A Language of Life* by Marshall B. Rosenberg
- *The Assertiveness Workbook* by Randy J. Paterson
- *The Assertiveness Guide for Women* by Julie de Azevedo Hanks

It is beyond the scope of this guide to go through all of the many communication styles. However, below are my top 10 recommendations for healthy communication.

1. Try family therapy.
If you do not feel safe with your mother, having a vulnerable dialogue will be exceptionally hard. Because of past attempts, you may not feel comfortable opening up to her. Family therapy can help create a safe foundation for vulnerable conversations, if both parties are willing to go.

Regardless if you attend family therapy or not, the following suggestions still apply.

2. Think before you speak.
You may want to journal or jot down some of your thoughts and feelings before you say them out loud, as it will help you express yourself with clarity. This is also helpful if you believe you may forget or get overwhelmed by emotions to speak clearly.

3. Own your feelings & speak in "I" statements.
For example, "I feel disappointed when you do this behavior," rather than "You make me feel disappointed..." No one is responsible for your feelings, and you are not responsible for anyone else's feelings. One can influence your emotions, but you are the only one in charge of your feelings.

4. Have self-respect & actionable requests.
Part of effective communication is having self-respect, which means honoring your thoughts, feelings, beliefs, and overall boundaries. Practicing effective communication is a way to stand up for yourself and set boundaries. You may also want to think about your actionable requests for your mother. Do you want her to take specific actions, or do you want acknowledgment of your feelings or an apology?

5. Speak to help the listener.
Be clear and straightforward with your statements, so the listener can better hear and understand you (if they want to hear and understand you).

6. Be empathetic & nonjudgemental.
Do not attack or name-call.
There is no need to shame someone for their behavior. It will only make them resentful or become triggered. For instance, you do not need

to call your mother "irresponsible," "neglectful," or "difficult" to express your feelings about her behaviors. As noted before, her behaviors can be "irresponsible," "neglectful," or "difficult," but that is not her identity.

7. Do not allow interruptions while you are speaking.

8. It takes two to communicate.
If your mother does not want to listen to you, that is on her. You are not responsible for her listening abilities. However, you can communicate how her behavior (of not listening or interrupting) makes you feel.

9. All behavior is communication.
For example, if someone hangs up on you while speaking to them on the phone, they communicate that they do not want to hear what you have to say. Hence, be mindful of your non-verbal communication (and your behavior towards others) because they also communicate information.

10. Listen to understand: power phrase and ask questions.
Powerphrasing what the person has just said will help you check that you understand them correctly. If you have questions, ask them.

Journal

1. What feelings or thoughts do you want to express to your mother?

2. What are your actionable requests? Do you want acknowledgment or apology?

3. Do you have any questions for your mother?

4. What do you want your nonverbal language or behaviors to communicate to her?

5. Does your mother interrupt you while you are trying to express yourself? If so, are you willing to tell her how her behaviors make you feel?

6. How do you feel about your level of self-respect? What has influenced your self-respect?

7. How have past attempts to communicate with your mother turned out? How has the past affected your communication with her now?

Journal

1. Where in the spectrum does your mother lie?

"Behaviors and Their Level of Difficulty Spectrum"
By Jasmine Cepeda, LCSW

Mildly   Moderately   Severely   Extremely

2. How do her behaviors make you feel?

3. Do you believe these feelings are "proportionate" and "rational" to the event? Why or Why Not?

4. How aware is she of her difficult behavior/s? And why do you think her level of awareness is so?

5. How willing is she to try to understand your perspective?

6.A. How willing do you think she is in trying to change or understand you?

B. What evidence do you have for your answer?

C. What other thoughts or feelings do you have about your answers above?

7. Are you in an abusive relationship with your mother? Why or why not?

8. If so, to what degree do you want your mother in your life?

9. Do you feel you have internalized some of your mother's manipulative, narcissistic, or distant tendencies? If so, what are your thoughts and feelings about this?

10. Describe the "ideal" level of distance that you want with your mother. (For example, how many hours or days can you see her in one week or month?

11. Is this the current state of affairs? If not, why not?

12. Do you think your mother may have a mental health disorder? Why or Why not?

#5. Identifying Your Triggers

Triggers may be a thing, behavior, or event that evokes distressing feelings. Sometimes triggers can also bring you back to traumatic feelings or events in your past.

It is vital to be aware of your triggers and to recognize why they are so provoking. Triggers usually mean more than what is on the surface. It may be helpful to explore your deeper thoughts or feelings that come up before, during, and after the trigger.

For example, the initiating event or behavior may be that your mother verbally attacks you about something or calls you negative names. The underlying feelings may be of insecurity, helplessness, fear, or sadness. The deep underlying thoughts may be: "My mother is so horrible, or "My mother wants to hurt me," or "It's not safe to be with my mother." And if you internalize her negative words, you may attack yourself with those same words: "I am worthless...I am a bad daughter..."

Sometimes your mother's presence can be a trigger and make you feel uncomfortable or anxious. This may be because she reminds you of the many times she has hurt you with her actions, and you have unprocessed and unresolved thoughts and feelings about her behavior.

Triggers may stem from the overall unpleasant feelings you have towards your mother's painful treatment—treatments like consistently judging or belittling you, or not respecting your boundaries.

Journal

1. What are the behaviors, sayings, or actions that your mother does that trigger you?

2. How do you usually feel before, during, and after?

3. What are some of your thoughts before, during, and after?

Journal

4. Have you told her these actions trigger or affect you? Why or why not?

5. Has she ever changed her behavior or apologized?

6. Is your mother's presence or being around her a trigger? If so, how, and what feelings/thoughts come up in her presence?

On Judgement Based on Gender, Sexuality, Color, & Body

Some harmful parts of the Latin-American culture include the machismo attitude, sexism, homophobia, racism, and unrealistic beauty standards. For example, what it means to be "masculine" or "feminine" or beautiful in Latin-American culture can often limit the expression and freedom of the individual. Moreover, these intense forms of discrimination can become violent and even deadly.

Men are expected to be "macho" and more aggressive and are often rewarded with these behaviors (sometimes even by other Latina/x folks that perpetuate the binary expressions of gender). Meanwhile, women are told to be subordinate, submissive, pure, and passive.

Men have just as little space to express their "feminine" emotions (sadness, joy, care), as women do to express their "masculine" emotions (and sexuality). Emotions are not meant to be defined as "feminine" or "masculine," but society's expectations on gender have pushed these ideas forward.

Latino/a/x parents can treat their children differently based on gender—babying the boys/men, while parentifying the girls/women with more responsibility, and higher expectations to be "dutiful," "pure," or "the perfect daughter."

Latino/a/x parents can also criticize their children, regardless of gender (but mostly their daughters), on their weight, body size, or form. They do not allow space for **body acceptance**.

Some parents may even hypersexualize their children early in their lives, which may give the children the false idea that their looks and body are all that matter.

Lastly, though Latinx folks come in all colors and skin tones, racism and colorism continue to permeate the culture and harm the self-esteem of many individuals. White or fair skin is seen as "better," and folks discriminate and judge others based on the darkness of their skin.

Journal

1. How has any unhealthy concepts of gender, sexuality, weight, body, beauty, or skin color affected:
A. your relationship with your mother?

B. your relationship with your father? (We will explore more on your father in Part 2).

C. how your mother treats each sibling?

D. your gender or sexuality expression? And expectations for others?

E. your self-esteem? And view on beauty, color, weight, etc.

2. What are your thoughts and feelings about the answers above?

Lo Que Nos Dicen

The stereotypes about Latina moms are that they can be overbearing, judgemental, and loud; and that they are always cleaning and cooking. All one has to do is look at the many Buzzfeed articles and videos on Latina moms to see examples (as shown below).

latina moms buzzfeed	🎤 🔍

Threats Latina Moms Say - BuzzFeed
https://www.buzzfeed.com › gadieldelorbe › threats-latina-moms-say ▾
Threats **Latina Moms** Say. "Me bajas el volumen o te cambio el tono." Posted on January 10, 2017, at 1:01 p.m.. Gadiel Del Orbe. **BuzzFeed** Motion Pictures ...

Latina Moms: Savage Moments - BuzzFeed
https://www.buzzfeed.com › gadieldelorbe › latina-moms-savage-moments ▾
Latina Moms: Savage Moments. "Esta Bueno Que Te Pase." Posted on May 28, 2017, at 10:01 a.m.. Gadiel Del Orbe. **BuzzFeed** Motion Pictures Fellow ...

Latina Moms: "Cuando Yo Me Muera" - BuzzFeed
https://www.buzzfeed.com › curlyvelasquez › latina-moms-cuando-yo-me-... ▾
Latina Moms: "Cuando Yo Me Muera". You're going to miss me... Posted on May 12, 2017, at 2:01 p.m.. Curly Velasquez. **BuzzFeed** Motion Pictures Staff ...

13 Reasons Why Latina Moms Must Be Protected ... - BuzzFeed
https://www.buzzfeed.com › toyotalatino › reasons-why-latina-moms-are-t... ▾

Most of the Buzzfeed articles and videos about Latina moms can be humorous and relatable. However, from my experience interviewing Latinx folks, there are also many harsh and mean things Latina moms often say to their children that are not funny. Below are some examples:

- ¡No sirves para nada!
- ¡Malagradecida/o¡
- ¡Eres una mal hija/o!
- ¡No sabes hacer nada!
- ¿Por qué estás llorando?

- ¡Eres tan estupida/o
- ¡Eres un idiota!
- ¡Sin vergüenza!

Unfortunately (and fortunately) for us, the bilingual brain works in mysterious ways. For example, if English is the language you primarily use to understand concepts and people, you may tend to think in English. Therefore, when you are having a conversation in Spanish, you may unconsciously translate Spanish into English to think clearly. For further reference, Albert Costa's *The Bilingual Brain: And What It Tells Us about the Science of Language* (2020) is a great read!

Some Latinx folks have shared with me during my group sessions that they often translate the harsh things their mothers say from Spanish into English, making them feel even worse! Grasping two sets of mean comments in two different languages can be overwhelming. For instance, the previous examples translate to:

- "You are useless!"
- "Ungrateful!"
- "You are a bad daughter/son!"
- "You don't know how to do anything!"
- "Why are you crying?"
- "You are so stupid!"
- "You are an idiot!"
- "You have no shame!"

You may not take your mother's harsh comments seriously, and you may find them humorous, but sometimes these negative comments can sneak into your unconscious and indeed make you feel "ashamed" and "bad," as she is saying. More on *internalization* will be examined later in this guide.

The harsh comments may have only occurred as a form of discipline, a method your mother may have learned from her caregivers. Empathy does not mean that you excuse her behavior but rather build more compassionate understanding. In Part 2, we will explore the importance of having compassion for your mother and her socio-historical-psychological background.

••••••••••••••••••••••

Journal

1. What are some harsh things that your Latina mother says to you in Spanish?

In English?

2. What are your **thoughts** about her sayings?

3. How do you **feel** about her harsh sayings? (feelings are emotional states, not thoughts)

4. What actions do you take? For instance, do you say harsh things back?

5. Connect your actions to your thoughts and feelings.

●●●●●●●●●●●●●●●●●●●●

Lost in Translation

Sadly, what often gets lost in translation is what we may want to say to our mothers. Like previously mentioned, if English is the language you use to express yourself the most, you may have trouble finding the right Spanish words to communicate with your mother effectively. If that is the case, having google translate on your side may be helpful!

However, there are levels to being bilingual. Depending on your abilities, you may be better at expressing yourself in Spanish or do well in both languages.

Also, it is great if your mother understands English and you can express yourself in English.

Journal

1. A. Do you have trouble speaking to your mother in Spanish?

B. In English?

C. How do you **feeling and thoughts** about this? (feelings are emotional states, not thoughts).

2. A. What sorts of things would you talk to her about if the language barrier did not exist?

B. How would things be different if she understood or spoke English (if she doesn't)?

Being the 1st Gen. Translator

Many first-generation or immigrant children complain about having to translate letters or phone calls for their parents. Parents may be too busy or stressed out with their jobs and raising a family to learn English.

However, taking on the role of translator for your mother/parents often changes the child-parent power dynamic. That is, they come to need you in a way that a child may not be ready to be needed.

Similarly, it may show the child the limits of their parent's competence, which may be too soon for a child to recognize. Unconsciously, most children like to see their parents as "superheroes" or individuals to look up to; hence, when they see the limits of their caregiver's abilities so early on, it can be disappointing (unconsciously or not).

Taking on the translator role also gives the kids leeway to lie to their parents concerning situations where English is needed to understand what is going on (i.e., in school).

Moreover, having parents who do not know the school or college admissions system in the US can be challenging. It may make their child become discouraged to apply to schools or highly self-reliant.

As adults, having your parents depend on you to translate things can be annoying and frustrating. You may resent them for not knowing English. However, as we will explore in Part 2, being empathetic towards your parents can help you forgive them for what they could not control.

Journal

1. Did you grow up translating letters or phone calls for your mother? If so, what are your thoughts and feelings about this?

2. Would you **always** do it for her? If you said no to her, how would she react?

3. Who else was around to help her?

4. Did you ever take advantage of her language limitations by lying to her about areas in your life? If so, what areas, and why?

5. Do you think her language limitation may have unconsciously affected your view of your mother?

6. Did your mother ever help you with school work, or your college admissions process?

7. As an adult, are you still her translator? If so, what are your **feelings and thoughts** about this?

Parentification in Your Immigrant Family

Having the "translator" role is only one way children (especially first-generation kids) can become *parentified*.

Parentification was first coined in 1965 by Hungarian-American psychiatrist Ivan Boszormeny-Nagu. He initially used the term to describe cases where parents use their children as substitutes or replacements for their missing parents. These parents expect their children to fulfill the needs that their parents did not meet.

In 1973, along with his colleague, Geraldine M. Spark, Boszormeny-Nagu elaborated on parentification as the unwanted and undeserved responsibility and pressure on a child to take care of their parents, siblings, or general household. As the parentified child, it becomes their job to help sustain the functioning of the family. It usually becomes an emotional weight that leads to feelings of resentment, anger, and sadness.

Boszormeny-Nagu and Spark also described parentification occurring when children meet their caregivers' emotional or psychological needs (usually unconsciously), like the need for distraction, relatedness, support, understanding, etc., (all the while, the child's emotional or psychological needs go unmet). In general, the parentified child's efforts go unappreciated and unrecognized (1973).

The researchers also explained that parentification could lead to some positive and beneficial consequences in adulthood, especially at work, in romantic relationships, or as a parent (Boszormeny-Nagu and Spark, 1973). Still, the adverse effects live on.

In my experience as a Therapist, I have noticed the heartbreaking pain that parentified children and adult children carry with them, especially from not having the experience of trusting their caregiver to be reliable and available, which is an experience many children naturally crave from their parents. The safety, innocence, and freedom that come with that security are missed. Even more troubling, I have noticed that some parentified adult children defend against this pain by normalizing and accepting this imbalanced relationship. With that dynamic, they learn not to need anything from their parents (but not without an emotional cost).

The need to feel free to need or rely on your parent is a need in and of itself. Whether folks repress it or not, this unmet need creates a lost childhood and lost relationship. Whether folks meet their needs elsewhere or become highly independent, not having the freedom to need their parent or rely on them is a loss that (like most lost things) needs to be mourned.

For kids in immigrant families and first-generation children, parentification may have been (and may continue to be) a requirement for the family's survival in a new country! It is understandable, especially when some families come from cultures (especially in their home countries) that necessitate the children to take on family responsibilities.

However, just because something makes sense does not mean its unpleasant consequences are invalid.

References:
Boszormenyi-Nagy, I. (1965). A theory of relationships: Experience and transaction. In I. Boszormenyi-Nagy & J. L. Framo (Eds.),Intensive family therapy: Theoretical and practical aspects (pp. 38-86). New York:Harper & Row.

Boszormenyi-Nagy, I., & Spark, G. M. (1973). Invisible loyalties: Reciprocity in intergenerational family therapy. Harper & Row.

Journal

1. Were you, or are you, a parentified child to your mother? If so, how?

2. How do you *feel* about this?

3. What are your **thoughts** about this?

4. Why do you think your mother parentified you? Did she not know English? Was she struggling? Was she depressed? Etc.

On Siblings

Every sibling reacts to their mother's difficult behaviors differently: some may withdraw or distance themselves, while others may attach themselves more—forming a co-dependent and abusing relationship.

As already mentioned, gender also plays a role in Latin American culture, regarding what is "acceptable" for a son versus a daughter. Siblings may feel upset about the freedom (or lack their of) that their other siblings may (or may not) have based on their gender. They may or may not express their resentment (and other feelings) towards their siblings or mother.

That being the case, having siblings can have its benefits. For example, you may vent about your mother to each other and feel solidarity. Your siblings may also stand up for you and be emotionally supportive and understanding.

Lastly, having a neglectful or manipulative mother can impair the self-esteem of all her children. For instance, a mother who openly compares the siblings to each other can cause self-doubt and low self-confidence in her children. It can also lead to an increase in sibling rivalry or antagonism within the siblings.

Journal

1. How do you feel about your relationship with your sibling/s?

2. How do your other sibling/s respond to your mother's challenging behaviors? How do you feel about this?

3. Has having had your sibling/s been beneficial for you? If so, how?

Sibling Abuse

A mother who fails to intervene with sibling bullying or abuse, hurts the self-worth of her children tremendously. Parents need to intercede when bullying or abuse between siblings occurs, so the bullying or abusive child can learn to process guilt and shame, and empathize with others. These children also needs to be closely attended to (in general), so they don't become accustomed to manipulating or abusing others (which can lead to criminal activity or the development of an anti-social personality).

Meanwhile, it's also important for the bullied or abused child to feel protected and validated by their parent, so they can learn to self-validate, stand up for themselves, and set boundaries. It's vital for a child's self-worth to feel protected by their parents—when that does not happen, the child may feel unworthy or not good (or important) enough for protection (which can lead them into abusive relationships in their adulthood). These traumatic sibling experiences can lead folks to feel ignored, dismissed, and neglected.

Journal

1. Have you experienced sibling bullying or abuse? If so, what memories are attached to your experience? What are your feelings and thoughts?

2. Did/does your mother compare or manipulate you and your siblings?

3. Did/does your mother neglect sibling bullying or abuse? If so, how do you feel about this?

4. If you are an only child: do you ever think your mother relies on you because you are "all she has?" If so, how do you feel about this?

Family Roles

Through her research with children of alcoholics, Wegscheider-Cruse (1981) coined six family roles. I will use her family roles to explain a dysfunctional family system. In general, the roles come from the family's need for stability, albeit through unhealthy relationships.

1. The **Dependent** (the person living with an addiction or addictive behavior)

2. The **Chief Enabler** (the person in denial or enabling the behavior of the dependent)

3. The **Hero** (the child who appears competent, serious, and overachieving may feel inadequate. This child is usually parentified)

4. The **Scapegoat** (the child that usually presents with defiant behaviors and attitudes. The family focuses the blame for problems on this child rather than the actual problem)

5. The **Lost Child** (the withdrawn child that tends to do solitary activities away from the family. They may not develop enough social skills and may overcompensate by having a very active fantasy life)

6. The **Mascot** (The child that provides humor and distraction for the family, although others cannot take them seriously. They bring relief to the family (Wegscheider-Cruse, 1981).

Journal

1. Can you relate to any of the family roles? Which one and why? What are your thoughts and feelings about this?

References:
Wegscheider-Cruse, S. (1981), *Another Chance: Hope and Health for the Alcoholic Family*, Palo Alto, CA: Science and Behavior Books.

#6. Identifying Your Unmet Childhood Needs

The psychological and emotional consequences of your mother's challenging behaviors needs to be processed.

Sometimes we may be in denial about our childhoods and lose sight of our unmet childhood needs. No parent is perfect, and it would be idealistic to think that parents can meet all your needs.

Caregivers are indeed responsible for meeting the basic survival needs of their children, including physiological, shelter, safety, and care. Many parents can be great at meeting the basic needs, like food and shelter, but struggle to meet the emotional needs of their children. Emotional needs include, but are not limited to: *acceptance, consistency, reliability, appreciation, respect, consideration, play, creativity, emotional safety, understanding, a sense of belonging, engaged interest, affection, positive attention, and encouragement.*

Safety and protection are needs that are meant to be "basic," but sometimes mothers struggle to keep their children safe 24/7 (especially if the child is physically or sexually abused). Moreover, if child abuse occurs within the family, some mothers protect the perpetrator and keep the abuse a secret because they are not mentally capable of handling it.

If your mother did not meet your need for safety, it might be why you do not know how to protect or defend yourself. She may have modeled to you how to be passive, helpless, or "without a voice."

Journal

1. Using the examples of needs listed on the previous page, what basic or emotional needs *did* your mother **meet** for you as a child?

(tip: google a list of more needs if you'd like)

2. What are your **thoughts** and **feelings** about this? (reminder: feelings are emotional states, not thoughts)

3. What basic or emotional needs *did she not* **meet?**

4. What are your **thoughts** and **feelings** about this?

5. Do you remember trying to meet the unmet needs on your own, with another caregiver, sibling, friend, teacher, or any other person around? If so, how were your needs met by yourself or this person? Find a photo of you and this person (if you have one) and reflect.

6. Do you remember feeling upset when your needs were unmet by mom or anyone else? If so, what memories or feelings come up?

7. A. If you were sexually or physically abused as a child, did your mother act towards protecting you? What are your thoughts and feelings about this?

Exploring Your Traumatized, Wounded Inner Child (or Mother Wound)

We all have an inner child inside of us. The inner child is the image or idea that we have of ourselves as children. If your childhood was positive, safe, and filled with emotionally attentive caregivers, you are lucky to have a pleasant inner child. However, if your childhood was unsafe, emotionally unavailable, cold, traumatizing, abusive, or neglectful, you may have a **deeply wounded inner child**.

Throughout this guide, we have been specifically exploring childhood wounds and traumas caused by your mother, or **your mother-wound**. However, other folks may have also caused your inner child wounds (leading to the "father wound" or "sibling wound"). I encourage you to seek therapy for these specific relationship traumas.

Some examples of traumatizing childhood experiences done by your mother include:

- ignoring, bullying, or belittling you
- shaming, criticizing, or humiliating you
- blaming you for her feelings or actions
- dismissing or invalidating your feeling
- guilt-tripping or manipulating you
- showing you conditional love and care
- being self-centered or lacking boundaries
- giving you adult responsibilities or duties
- intentionally (or not) withdrawing, rejecting, or leaving you (for example: giving you the "cold shoulder" to "punish you")
- being disengaged or disinterested in your feelings, desires, or life outside of the home
- being physically unsafe or not physically protecting you (leading to physical or sexual abuse)

69

If you grew up with a mother who did not accept or respect you as a unique, separate self or a mother who emotionally abandoned you if you did not please her, you might fear others will do the same to you as an adult. You may fear rejection or abandonment, which may cause you to struggle with the following:

- People-please, setting boundaries, saying no, fear of judgment, & social anxiety
- Not asking for (or knowing) what you want
- Self-doubt & low self-worth
- An excessive need for external validation, attention, or approval
- Fear of failure or success (because it may trigger your mother who is self-centered or only shows interest if you are exceptional or "the best")
- Imposter-syndrome and low self-esteem (because you have internalized your mother's shaming and criticizing messages)
- Not knowing your true/authentic self or your true preferences (because your mother has taught you to put her needs and wants [and others'] before your own)
- Trouble asking for help & trusting others (because your mother was unreliable or shamed you when you asked for help)
- Being too self-reliant, controlling, or a perfectionist (because your mother parentified you
- Having abusive romantic relationships (like you have with your mother)
- Low interest in others & low interest in your own emotions or thoughts (because those were the behaviors modeled to your by your mother)

- **Lack of self-care** (through risk-taking or irresponsible behaviors: such as binge-eating, self-harm, substance abuse, or addiction) and may be caused by wanting to be rebel from an overly-responsible childhood

No childhood (or mother) is perfect (and we will discuss this in more depth in the next chapter). However, having a deep mother wound can be so pain-provoking that you may begin to resent your mother for her neglect and abuse. You may also start to feel angry that you have to do things like spend time and emotional labor processing your childhood, spend money on therapy, and "do the work" to heal your inner child. **All of your feelings are valid.** You have the right to feel frustrated that you did not get the emotional support you deserved as a child and now need to do the hard work of processing and mourning your past. Take time to validate your resentment, anger, frustration (and ultimately) sadness, and grief.

●●●●●●●●●●●●●●●●●●●●●

Journal

1. What are some of your inner childhood wounds or traumas that have affected your relationship with your mother? What are your thoughts and feeling about your mother wound?

Understanding the Power of Attachment

Babies need to feel secure in their caregiver's ability to meet both their **basic needs** (food, shelter, safety, etc.) and **emotional needs** (comfort, care, attention, etc.). If the baby does not feel secure, they will form *insecure attachments*.

For instance, babies know that they depend on their caregivers for all of their needs. Babies know that if their caregivers are physically absent, they will not survive. They also know that they will not survive if their caregivers do not respond to their crying (or emotions). Hence, babies enter **survival mode** when they do not sense physical or emotional security. They unconsciously find a way to attach to their caregiver (even in unsafe and unstable circumstances). To maintain the relationship and get at least some of their needs met, babies learn to insecurely attach (Ainsworth et al, 1978; Bowlby, 1969).

Researchers have described such insecure attachments towards caregivers as: **ambivalent** (or anxious), **avoidant**, or **disorganized** (Ainsworth et al, 1978; Bowlby, 1969).

An infant or child with an **ambivalent** (or *anxious*) attachment may have mixed feelings about their caregiver and behave inconsistently because of their caregiver's *inconsistencies* (sometimes attentive and warm, sometimes neglectful and indifferent). The child can appear nervous, insecure, impulsive, clingy, and have trouble focusing (Ainsworth et al, 1978). When the caregiver appears cold, the child may fear that their caregiver will "stop loving me," which may cause the child to "try to get their love back" in unhealthy ways (like crying, yelling, having a tantrum, or pleasing their parent).

72

A child with an **avoidant** attachment will not show much emotion towards their caregiver and avoid affection or closeness. Because their caregiver is emotionally unavailable, distant, or passive, the child responds with the same emotional distance. The child represses their deep desire for emotional connection and may deny their sadness over not having said intimacy. They may also fear rejection and suffer from emotional isolation. These kids also start to believe that others cannot be relied on (Ainsworth et al, 1978).

A child with a **disorganized** attachment may have paradoxical ways of behaving, and relate to their caregiver based off **fear**. The child is confused and apprehensive about going to their caregiver for comfort because they are *unpredictable*, going from caring (safe) to **terrifying** (not safe). They may approach strangers in their attempt to find safety. And sadly, they may be manipulated by adults because they are so vulnerable. The child can appear depressed, angry, or passive (Ainsworth et al, 1978).

A baby or child who grows up with an insecure attachment may form coping strategies to relieve their anxiety (such as crying, having outbursts, being distant, or having obsessive behaviors, like biting nails, skin-picking, pulling hair, etc.) These coping styles, be them "difficult" for the caregiver as they may be, are attempts to get some of their needs (like attention, comfort, or space) met. Sadly, parents who are not attuned to their child's needs may be blocked by their childhood traumas to tune in.

References
Ainsworth, M. D. S., Blehar, M. C., Waters, E., & Wall, S. (1978). Patterns of attachment: A psychological study of the strange situation. Oxford, England: Lawrence Erlbaum.
Bowlby, J. (1969). Attachment and loss: Vol. I. Attachment. New York: Basic Books.

Journal

1. What was your attachment style with your mother as a child? Why do you think it was this way?

• • • • • • • • • • • • • • • • • • • •

Adult attachment is highly affected by your childhood attachment to your caregiver. Labels to describe adult, insecure attachments include dismissive, fearful, and preoccupied (Bartholomew & Howowitx, 1991).

An adult with a **preoccupied attachment** may be overly invested and dependent on others for their self-worth and love (because their caregiver did not provide enough of either). They desperately want others to provide the attention and love that they feel they need and deserve and react in extreme ways (resentful or angry) when others do not meet their high, unrealistic expectations. They also worry about abandonment and rejection (Bartholomew & Howowitx, 1991).

An adult with a **dismissive attachment** style may deny dependency on others and become highly self-reliant. They may minimize or devalue the importance of relationships and avoid intimacy. They may develop this attachment style because they learned that their caregiver was not consistently reliable (Bartholomew & Howowitx, 1991).

An adult with a **fearful attachment** style may avoid closeness, but not because they devalue relationships like dismissive attachment. Instead, they avoid intimacy because they fear they are not "loveable" or worthy (thus, they also fear rejection) (Bartholomew & Howowitx, 1991). They fear others will hurt them because of these self-defeating beliefs. They might believe things like: "I'm so stupid, no wonder they cheated on me." They may have had a disorganized childhood attachment to their caregiver.

Ideally, we want secure attachments where we can trust the other person in the relationship to be reliable and responsive to our interpersonal needs. When we do not get that, we behave in ways that, ironically so, decrease emotional closeness.

● ●

Journal

1. What is your adult attachment to your mother now? Why do you think it is this way?

2. What is your attachment style towards others (friends, romantic partners, etc.)? Why do you think it is this way?

References
Bartholomew, K., & Horowitz, L. M. (1991). "Attachment styles among young adults: A test of a four-category model." Journal of Personality and Social Psychology, 61(2), 226-244.

Attachment, Trauma Bonding, & Abuse

Often, folks may unconsciously seek romantic partners that will perpetuate their insecure attachment styles. These folks unconsciously choose partners with personality traits or behaviors similar to their caregivers, which continues their insecure attachment style. They may feel "intense chemistry" with a person, but in reality, it may just be the *insecure attachment that the person is triggering* that is **familiar**. Many folks can even get *addicted* to their insecure attachment styles simply because they do not know any other way to attach.

An extreme version of this form of addiction can be seen in **trauma bonding**. Trauma bonding is akin to *Stockholm Syndrome*, wherein folks begin to feel trust, affection, and dependence on the very person causing them pain. It is a type of **survival** strategy and can be seen in toxic and abusive relationships.

Many types of manipulation, including in trauma bonding, are maintained by the abuser's power within the **cycle of abuse**. The cycle of abuse includes the three main phases: tension building, explosion, and honeymoon. The abuser's power is supported by the victim's *denial* and *isolation* (Walker, 1979).

It is helpful to identify your attachment style with your mother to understand your relationship better and learn how to build more secure, healthy attachments with others. Therapy is a practical first step in developing the insight to help you change.

Reference:
Walker L. (1979). *The Battered Woman*. New York, NY: Harper & Row

Journal

1. Do you think you have (unconsciously) sought romantic partners that have perpetuated your insecure attachment style? Explain.

Watching Your Defense Mechanisms

Every child responds to their mother's problematic or distant/disengaged behaviors differently. As we can see, the instinctual need for emotional support and connection sometimes leads us to attach to our caregivers in unhealthy ways.

Every person also has **defense mechanisms**: psychological processes, usually unconsciously started, to defend against, or avoid distressing feelings or anxiety. Hence, any behavior can be a defense, and there are an infinite amount of defenses. Defense mechanisms arise as survival tactics to maintain our psychological equilibrium (*it is often part of the healing process to thank our defenses for protecting us, as we try to let them go*).

Folks with difficulties relating to their mother may practice multiple defense mechanisms, including: dissociation, lying, omitting, fantasy, repression, denial, avoidance, humor, regression, projection, obsessing, controlling, over-working, under-working, over-eating, under-eating,

over-sharing, over-explaining, over-exposing self, drinking, smoking, numbing, distractions, intellectualization, overcompensation, under-compensation, over-identification (with the mother), rationalization (of her negative behaviors), and/or turning anger, hatred, or any distressing emotions (that they have about their mom) towards self, self-mutilation, etc.

For example, when folks grow up with a mother who is emotionally distant or has depression, as children, they may not understand that their mother's behaviors are not personal. Hence, they may resent her or think that she does not want to attend to them. They may **internalize** the interpretations and believe: "I am unworthy of attention," or, "No one loves me..." To defend against feeling forgotten, unloved, or lonely, they may **overcompensate** in school by being the fun, outgoing, or intelligent child. In school, they may finally get the attention they so desperately want. Then, in adulthood, the person may view their success in school as a large part of their sense of self and worth. The overcompensating behaviors act as a defense against the idea that they are unloved or unwanted (which all stem from their mother's disengaged behaviors).

Another example is when children grow up with caregivers who suffer from other mental health or substance abuse disorders. In some cases, the child may react to their mother's need for help by caring for her and becoming "parentified." The "little parent" role is a way to defend against feeling helpless and scared. This care-taking role is not a role that a child is meant to have, and the habit can sometimes lead to **over-controlling or obsessive behaviors**. Sadly, the child may lose their desire for play, and chance to be carefree, along with other unmet needs. As adults, the care-taking habit can also be taken advantage of by others, like romantic partners.

Other folks may use drugs, alcohol, food, work, sex or other distractions to avoid their feelings.

Meanwhile, some folks may deny their true desires and feelings and live their entire lives seeking their mother's approval, all to feel "good enough" in her eyes (even if just for a moment). They lose sight of their true interests, goals, and values and do what their mother wants.

••••••••••••••••••••

Journal

1. Using the defenses listed, what were/are some of your defense mechanisms towards your mother's difficult behaviors?

2. What are your thoughts and feelings about your defenses?

3. Take a moment to thank your defenses for helping you survive!

Part 2
Remothering Yourself & Self-Protection

Part 2 is all about compassion, self-protection, and **self-preservation**. It's about meeting your unmet needs and taking responsibility for your life. It is also about forgiveness, kindness, respect, and gratitude towards yourself, but especially your mother. I hope you will find deep meaning, resilience, and strength in these next set of practices!

#7. Leaning Towards A More Compassionate Narrative

I hope you have learned the importance of building self-validation by verbalizing your true feelings and thoughts about your mother.

As noted, unconsciously or not, you have created a narrative (or meaning) from these feelings and thoughts. Whether the meaning is based on a false interpretation or is entirely correct, I hope you have gained insight into why you have this narrative, so that you can begin to let go of it and create a more empathetic one.

The meaning or story that you make of your mother's behaviors is often the root cause of your distressing feelings towards her, hence the importance of letting go of it. Again, as stated in "#3 Accepting Ambivalence," letting go of the disempowering narrative does not excuse your mother for her behavior. However, it provides you with the ability to create a more empowering meaning with self-compassion, courage, and empathy.

The Socio-Historical-Psychological Context

Maintaining awareness of the external factors that have affected your mother's behaviors can help you build more empathy for her.

In Part 1, we slowly explored some of the socio-historical contexts of your mother's difficult behaviors (living in the machismo culture, your father's behaviors, etc.).

We also highlighted the possibility that she may have emotional issues that make her more fragile than others. Her profound, psychological dilemmas may come from her past trauma/s with her caregivers, physical, sexual, or verbal abuse, or trauma/stress from immigrating to the US, along with economic hardship.

Moreover, your mother may have many psychological complexes, including the belief that trauma is shameful (which often is a way to blame the victim) and should not be discussed (reinforcing one's shame and guilt). She may be passing down intergenerational or collective trauma (unconsciously) that you do not want to continue!

What's more, because of our patriarchal society, she may have an unhealthy need for "male" love or the "male gaze," which you may also want to work on (regardless of gender or sexuality).

She may also have an unhealthy need to maintain a "perfect" outside self-image or image of her life, which (again), she may have passed down to you.

The examples above may lead her to pressure you to live up to the image she wants you to be or that she wants others to see.

"I Don't Want to Love Her."

The trauma your mother has gone through may cause her to distance herself from loving you as deeply as you deserve. For instance, I had a client once explain to me why she was so emotionally withdrawn from her daughter. She was a survivor of sexual abuse and shared: "Every time I look at my daughter, it reminds me of what happened to me as a child... If I loved her with all of my heart, and something horrible happened to her, I would die!" This client feared that she would not be able to protect her daughter from the horrors of the world. Moreover, she struggled with having a deep love for her, since it triggered her trauma.

It is heartbreaking to (unconsciously or not) experience the effects of your mother's trauma. Of course, your mother can heal from her abusive past and give herself the freedom to love as deeply as she deserves, but she must do the work herself. Sadly, processing trauma can be so challenging that folks may avoid the work. Moreover, not having felt protected or safe as a child, mothers who have childhood trauma may not know how to meet their own protection needs and thus, not know how to protect their child.

Journal

1. Journal/free-write about the socio-historical-psychological context that makes your mother who she is today:

2. Journal/free-write about your ability to have empathy for your mother?

3. Do you believe that she has passed down any behaviors or belief systems onto you? Explain.

Find a picture/s of your mother when she was younger (before she was a mother) and paste it below.

What Are Her Unmet Needs?

Your mother's own unmet needs and emotional instability are most likely the cause of her problematic behaviors. Thus, it is essential to be conscious and empathetic to her needs, though you are not responsible for meeting her needs (only she is).

Once you become more conscious of what is going on when she behaves in her challenging ways, you can empathize and not internalize her negative comments and actions.

It can be challenging to be compassionate towards your mother when she has hurt you so much. However, increasing your understanding and empathy is a way to remind yourself that your mother does not behave in these ways because "you are a bad daughter," or "horrible son," or whatever she claims, but rather because of her emotional struggles.

For example, your mother may try to bully, manipulate, control, guilt-trip, or judge you over how you are living your life. These problematic behaviors may stem from her unmet needs for comfort, connection, a sense of relevance, control, etc.

This is not an excuse for her behavior, and you are not responsible for meeting her needs. Still, it is essential to bring empathy and awareness to her problematic behaviors so that you do not take them personally. You must act towards your self-protection, fulfillment, and desires, not her wishes.

Your mother is just like everyone else, a human being with her unique flaws and way of being. Your mother's challenging behaviors are not about you and all about her.

Though she may try to blame you for her actions, or project her negative feelings onto you, you must train yourself to remember that the challenging behaviors and unpleasant feelings are hers, not yours. She is the only one that must take accountability for her actions, feelings, and their consequences.

Focusing on having compassion for your mother's inability to fulfill her own needs can help you depersonalize the triggering incidents and decrease your distressing thoughts and feelings.

• •

Journal

1. What do you think are the unmet needs in your mother's life? Explain.

2. How do you feel about your mother's lack of fulfillment?

3. What, if any, are the obstacles between you and letting go of the responsibility to meet your mother's needs?

#8 Remothering Your Wounded Inner Child (Healing Your Mother Wound)

Remothering (or reparenting) is about acknowledging the emotions and experiences of your inner child. The good news: you have already been remothering yourself by practicing skills #1-6. Through #1. self-tending and #2. regulating your emotions, you have been validating the emotions of your inner child. By #3. accepting ambivalence and #4. practicing effective communication, you have been teaching yourself (and by proxy, your inner-child) about the importance of accepting the gray areas in life, as well as how to communicate effectively. Lastly, by #5. identifying your triggers, and #6. identifying your unmet childhood needs and inner wounds, you have increased your ability to grow and be an emotionally mature, aware, and stable adult.

Another way to reparent yourself is by practicing self-compassion. Luckily, you have just explored #7 feeling compassion for your mother, which will help you empathize with yourself. You can practice self-compassion by talking to yourself with a nurturing voice or as you would to a friend. Speaking to yourself with a comforting voice will help you be less critical, judgmental, and harsh towards yourself. Moreover, having empathy for yourself is crucial because it can help decrease your mother's ability to "guilt-trip" or manipulate you.

You can also reparent yourself through active imagination—imagine yourself as the grown adult you are today, soothing your inner child and meeting their unmet needs (sometimes it is helpful to pick a specific memory or age). By responding to these unmet needs (or childhood wounds), you are making peace with the pain that your inner child has gone through.

Journal

1. What may be some obstacles in remothering yourself as an adult (or meeting your unmet childhood needs)?

2. What may be some obstacles to seeing yourself as worthy and good enough to have your needs met?

3. Through meeting our own needs, we learn the importance of boundaries and valuing the needs of others. What are your thoughts and feelings concerning how you have respected the needs of others (such as friends, partners, co-workers, etc.)?

Journal

4. I believe self-affirmations are the most useful when you create your own! Create the unique self-affirmations that speak to you:

5. Paste a photo of you as a happy child below. Remember that this child is special, and you still have the power to heal from inner child wounds!

Taking Care of My Childhood Self

Meeting Your Adult Needs: Becoming Your True Self

Reparenting also means meeting your adult needs. By meeting your needs, you free up space to get closer to your authentic self, the true self that you hid to survive your dysfunctional family dynamics. Being free from negative internalized messages, beliefs, and others' desires empowers you to live based on **your** values and wants

Journal

Look back at "#6 Identifying Your Unmet Childhood Needs." Those exact unmet childhood needs you have identified are the same ones you need to try to provide yourself (except your interpersonal needs that are fulfilled in relationships or community).

For example, if your childhood needs for "play" or to "be carefree" went unmet, you can brainstorm ways you can "play" or be "carefree" as an adult (responsibly, of course). Or, if your need for safety and protection went unmet, you can provide yourself with those needs as an adult by decreasing risky behavior. Or if you feel your need for rest went unmet, you can plan moments and days of relaxation as an adult, etc.

1. How will you meet your adult needs that went unmet as a child?

#9 Setting EMOTIONAL & PHYSICAL Boundaries

Boundaries are crucial in relationships because they create realistic expectations, assure safety, and allow you to attend to your needs while being authentic to your true desires. Needs, such as space, comfortability, safety, etc., are important in relationships and necessary to feel mutually respected.

It is vital to set and maintain boundaries with your mother, especially if her difficult behaviors compromise your safety, self-respect, and self-worth.

Though you may indeed "feel bad" (which is not actually a feeling) for your mother, or indeed feel guilty, it is a form of self-protection to put your own emotional and physical needs first and "feel bad" for yourself! It's okay to feel pity or sympathy for your mother and not act on it. Every feeling does not require an action.

For example, just because your mother says she is "lonely," it does not mean you need to involve her in everything you do or that she can force herself into your day-to-day life. If she is indeed lonely, your mother is the only one responsible for meeting her own needs for social support.

If you do not believe your mother will realistically stop or ever change her challenging behaviors, then you must set both emotional and physical boundaries.

Self-tending, practicing effective communication, and re-mothering yourself are three ways to describe emotional boundaries; thus, practicing these strategies will create emotional boundaries.

93

Emotional boundaries are about protecting your heart. In general, boundaries are not about avoiding your mother, but rather, making sure you do not leave yourself vulnerable to her painful behavior. If she walks all over your boundaries, or is disrespectful and inconsistent, you cannot allow yourself the emotional space to be vulnerable with your mother. Vulnerability is something we save for those who value our boundaries and respect us.

Physical boundaries can be created by deciding when you will see your mother and for how long.

Some examples of what emotional or physical boundaries may look like are: keeping conversations superficial, not telling her about things she may be critical of, or misunderstand, limiting the amount of time spent with her to the number of minutes or hours you can handle, doing something convenient for the both of you (like errands or shopping).

You are no longer a child and are in control of your life and how you would like to spend your time. You have the right to decide the degree to which you want your mother in your life. You owe yourself the protection and consideration you did not have as a child.

Above all else, you may feel uncomfortable allowing your mother to see the authentic, full version of yourself because of her unpleasant reactions when you are yourself. This is very sad, but what remothering, self-tending, and meeting your needs means. Feeling and accepting the sadness that your mother will never know the authentic version of who you are is heartbreaking, but a consequence of her behavior. She gets the edited version of you, while you hold your tongue about what's really going on in your life. It may be hard to share with her both your joys and disappointments because in either case, she may somehow make you feel worse, make it about herself, or be unhelpful. Because she does not make it safe for you to open up, she does not get the privilege of knowing you (or bonding).

You do not have to cut your mother off completely to find relief. However, if you feel it is necessary to stop seeing or talking to your mother entirely, that is a valid route, especially if she is abusive.

Journal

1. What emotional boundaries will you create with your mother?

2. What physical boundaries will you create? I.e., How often/how long are you thinking of seeing her, and what are you willing to do with her?

3. Do you feel that the "no contact" path is necessary? If so, why?

Gaining Your Power Back & Out of the Repetition

There may be a cyclical and repetitive pattern that occurs with you and your mother. It may often have "dormant" periods wherein everything appears to be stable and fine, and you may let your guard down. However, an incident that has been bubbling can arise, and she may get upset with you, lash out, and you may get hurt all over again! Unfortunately, you may never be able to let your guard down!

When your mother puts you in a position where everything you do is "wrong" or "your fault," she is putting you in a position where you will never feel good or worthy enough. To feel good or worthy enough, you may appease her and do what she wants, trying to get the "high" of being on her "good side"—even if it's just for a moment—you compromise your self-respect and self-worth. This cycle of abuse is toxic and gives her the power and control that she is seeking while you remain vulnerable, powerless, and out of control.

The rejection hurts because all you want is to feel unconditionally accepted by your mother, but, sadly, her desire to get what she wants may be stronger than her ability to meet her child's emotional needs.

Rather than repeating the cycle over and over, maintaining your physical and emotional boundaries may be the best way out of the repetitive loop.

Keep Your Guard Up!

I want to help you gain insight into why you may struggle to maintain your boundaries (a.k.a consequences) for your mother's challenging behaviors.

Often, the sadness and pain of not having a deeper relationship with your mother may be the reason why you continue to hold out hope. However, as previously noted, it is vital to your remothering and safety to keep your guard up and not leave yourself vulnerable to her distressing behavior. Unfortunately, you may never trust her enough to reduce or remove the boundaries, so the boundaries may begin to define the relationship. But, fortunately, you will be increasing your self-respect and self-worth while learning how to meet your own needs.

Some folks also have trouble creating and maintaining boundaries with their mothers because they can not let go of the **fantasy** that their mothers will change. They may also hold on to the idea that their mother will "finally love me," "finally validate me," "finally respect me," "finally see my worth," and "finally think I'm special." **You are loveable, you are worthy, and you are special.** You cannot afford to give your mother this much power—power over your worth and value—especially if your fantasy will never be reality!

Sadly, practicing **effective communication** with your mother (i.e., calmly talking to your mother about how you feel about her and your boundaries), can turn into an argument (or cause you harm), since she may not respect you. Therefore, you do not have to tell her you are setting boundaries directly; you can do it slowly, so she does not get upset if it occurs abruptly. You have the right to guard (or protect) yourself.

Journal

1. Why do you think you have trouble creating or maintaining your boundaries with your mother?

2. Do you believe you can continue to try to get better at maintaining your boundaries? If so, explain why you believe in yourself!

3. Do you feel more comfortable practicing effective communication with your mother and talking to her about why you are setting your boundaries? Why or why not?

#10. Letting Go & Grieving Your "Fantasy Mom"

Ideally, you may have liked your mother to be "like the moms on TV," but that's not reality. Not that there can't be great moms in real-life! On the contrary, seeing a friend's mom or how your Aunt treats her children may show you that real life moms can be even better than TV moms! But it's unhealthy to idealize both examples of "perfect moms" since the day-in and day-out experiences with these moms can never be known (since you aren't their child). Still, some people compare "perfect moms" to their moms and get jealous, or begin to fantasize about a "perfect mom." Some folfs simply fantasize about a "better" mom.

Letting go and grieving your "fantasy mom" is one of the most sorrowful parts of healing—it means **fully accepting reality** and the dissatisfying relationship you have with your mother. It also means **letting go of the unrealistic expectation** that she will one day be the mother you always wanted. Unfortunately, the past is far behind you, and her chance to mother you when you needed it the most (as a child), is gone.

Releasing and mourning your "fantasy mom" also means letting go of the unrealistic expectation that she will one day be the mother you always wanted. It's about being **present** with what you do or don't have **right now** and accepting that, (even though it causes discomfort). **When you are finally able to move on from the past and not project into the future, you will be able to find comfort in the here and now.**

Grieving your lost childhood is complex, which is why I highly encourage therapy.

Journal

1. As a child, did you ever fantasize about having a "better mom?" If so, what was she like?

2. Do you think you still hold a "fantasy" version of your mother? If so, do you think you are ready to let her go, grieve her, and accept your mother for who she is today?

#11 Acceptance & Setting Realistic Expectations

We may have high expectations of our mothers, just as they may have high expectations of us as their children. We may be critical of them, just as they may be critical of us. Getting disappointed with others is inevitable because no one is perfect. With that said, just as you may like your mother to have more realistic expectations of who you are, it may be helpful to also set realistic expectations of who she is.

This may dishearten you because you may have positive and hopeful expectations for your mother, but setting realistic expectations is important, just as letting go of your "fantasy mom."

For example, if your mother has never said sorry to you, you should not expect her to say sorry to you in the future. It may be great if she does, and it would be a nice surprise, but it may be more helpful to expect her to be who she's already shown herself to be.

You can expect her difficult behavior, but you do not have to accept it. By maintaining your boundaries, you show her that there are consequences for her actions. But if she does make positive changes, that's great too, but you should not expect it.

Setting realistic expectations and accepting your mother in all her flaws can feel like you are "giving up on her." However, what you may really be giving up on is the idea that you have control to change her. We "give up" on things that are in our control, like a job, hobby, or belief. Thus, the sadness or helplessness that may come from feeling that you are "giving up" on your mother, might actually be the heartache that comes with letting go of a false sense of control over her. She's the only one who can change herself.

Something you do have control over is your boundaries and communication. These are coping strategies that are for you but that may also help your mother change. Still, you are not in direct control over your mother's changes. You share with her the control over the quality of the relationship (which is why you're reading this book), but she has authority over her part.

Ultimately, you do not have to "give up on your mother." You may not have the ideal relationship you would want with her, but you can still have a relationship. By having realistic expectations of her, you can expand your ability to see her positive traits and be grateful for them: maybe she cooks for you, or you enjoy doing a particular activity with her, or she makes you laugh with her funny stories, etc., Nonverbal gestures, like hugging, smiling, laughing, etc., can also be mutually pleasant.

Journal
Free-write about the attributes you enjoy about your mother?

On Forgiveness & Practicing Gratitude

You do not need an apology from your mother to forgive her or heal, especially since you might never get one. Because of their pride or fear of vulnerability, many mothers who engage in challenging behaviors do not accept accountability for their actions. Some don't even think that they've done anything wrong. Hence, you might never get an apology.

She may never change, but you can! If you have gone this far in this guide, I hope you have already seen that you have the agency and ability to stand up for yourself, even when it is hard! You have already come so far in this marathon! Don't "give up" on yourself! You have the empathy and self-awareness to take the next steps and practice forgiveness!

Forgiveness is not for her, and it is not an excuse for her behavior; it is so you can bring peace into your life and grow from a softer, resilient, and healthier place. If you feel the need, you may also want to forgive yourself for how you may have treated your mother.

Additionally, practicing gratitude can help you expand your perspective and let go of unrealistic expectations for your mother.

Journal

Free-write about your ability to forgive your mother (and yourself).

Journal

Free-write about what you are grateful for regarding your mother.

"I Don't Want to Become Like Her!"

The fear that you will become like your mother is understandable since one-way folks may defend against their mother's negative traits is to 1) deny them and then 2) unconsciously internalize them.

Folks may deny that the unpleasant traits exist in their mother because of the discomfort it causes them to think of their mother (who is supposed to protect and comfort them) as their source of pain.

By repressing their unpleasant emotions, they only feel pleasant emotions about their mother. All the while, they turn the negative feelings they do indeed feel about their mother onto themselves (disliking themselves).

To go further and create "evidence" for why they "do not like themselves," they may begin to act out their mother's negative traits and behaviors— behaving in such unpleasant ways themselves.

In the end, they think: "I am just like my mother." Another way to describe the phenomena is *identification with the aggressor* (Ferenczi, 1933).

Therefore, one way to make sure you do not become like your mother is to acknowledge your mother's unpleasant traits or challenging behaviors and accept your unpleasant feelings about her, rather than ignoring or internalizing them.

Reference: Ferenczi S. Confusion of tongues between adults and the child (1933). In: Balint M, ed. Final contributions to the problems and methods of psycho-analysis. London: Hogarth; 1955. pp. 156–67.

Journal

Can you relate to the fear, "I don't want to become like her?" If so, how?

• • • • • • • • • • • • • • • • • • • •

On Taking Care of Her When She Ages

To whatever extent you want to help your mother as she ages (financially or physically), it is your choice. It would be best if you did not let her control your decision through any form of guilt-tripping.

Journal:

To what extent do you think you will help your mother as she ages? How do you feel about this? What are your thoughts?

On Mourning Her in The Future

By the time your mother is no longer around, you would have known multiple versions of her, and if she is lucky, she would have known the many versions of you too!

You would have seen her as the mother who raised you, the mother she was to you as a teenager and an adult, and, si Dios quiere, you may even see her as a grandmother (or into her old age)!

Moreover, through your increased empathy for her, I hope you also get to see her as a human being—a woman, wife, friend, sister, employee, etc.

One day she will no longer be around, and it will break your heart. Regardless of how she has treated you, her impact on your life will be one of the grandest.

It is possible that in the future, the grief may hit you less hard than its potential because you took the initiative (now) to work on your unprocessed emotions and thoughts about your mother, so give yourself appreciation for your hard work!

As previously suggested, your mother may never change how she relates to you, but you have the power to change how you relate to her—and in that way, you have the strength to let go of your resentment.

When she is gone one day, at least you can say that she helped you tremendously in your self-growth. At least you can say she aided in your understanding of the profound influence that one person can have on your life.

#12. Meeting Your Interpersonal Needs: Building Deep Relationships With Others

As highlighted many times in this guide, interpersonal needs are crucial for individuals to feel a human connection and a greater sense of meaning in their life. Friendships, partnerships, and community are spaces to find deep connections and feel a sense of belonging! Now that you have a clearer sense of how you will cope with your mother's inability to meet your needs, you can meet these needs elsewhere.

• • • • • • • • • • • • • • • • • • • •

Journal

1. What basic or emotional needs do you need from your mother now, as an adult, that you think she is **capable** of meeting?

2. How do you know when other folks in your life (friends, partners, communities, etc.) are meeting your interpersonal needs? (Whatever your answer, this is what you should look for in relationships outside of your mother).

3. Brainstorm other ways your interpersonal needs can be met outside of your mother.

4. Journal about how this guide has affected your relationship roles (as a romantic partner, sibling, friend, etc.)

5. Journal about how this guide has affected your decision-making regarding
A. choice in partner

B. decision to have kids or not

C. or how you parent your children.

I am Worthy & Enough!

1. Journal about how this guide has affected your Self-Worth/ Self-Acceptance/ Self-Reliance/ Self-Protection/ Self-Compassion, etc.

2. Journal about how this guide has changed your relationship with your mother:
A. Your **feelings** about her?

B. Your **thoughts** about her?

C. And how you **act** with her.

D. Connect your actions to your feelings and thoughts.

3. On the next page, write a letter to your mom about all that you have discovered from this guide, Do not forget to express both your pleasant and unpleasant feelings, your triggers, and be empathetic. **Do not give your mother this letter.** The purpose of the letter is to help you internalize your growth and understand your new narrative. Your mother may not be ready for such a letter (or be emotionally capable). If you do ever want to give her the letter, I encourage you to attend therapy **first**.

Dear Mom,

Conclusion

I hope that you have grown the self-love and self-validation that you deserve! I hope you have accepted that you are special and absolutely worthy of getting your needs met! I hope you have fully accessed your resilience and strength and can finally flourish in all your potentiality and authenticity!

I also hope you will carry your re-mothering skills onward and continue to practice compassion for yourself, your mother, and others.

The "work" in healing will always be an ongoing process. All of the insight and new ways of being that you have built will continue to be strengthened with continued practice!

12 Ways to Cope With
Your Latina Mom & Her Difficulties

#1 Your Self-Tending Routine

#2 Feeling Your Feelings & Self Soothing/Regulating

#3 Accepting Ambivalence: Letting Go of the "She's All Bad" Narrative

#4 Practicing Effective Communication

#5 Identifying Your Triggers

#6 Identifying Your Unmet Childhood Needs

#7 A More Compassionate Narrative

#8 Re-mothering Your Wounded Inner Child (Healing Your Mother Wound)

#9 Setting EMOTIONAL & PHYSICAL Boundaries

#10 Letting Go & Grieving Your "Fantasy Mom"

#11 Acceptance & Setting Realistic Expectations

#12 Meeting Your Interpersonal Needs

Also by Jasmine Cepeda:

12 Ways to Cope With Your Latino Dad & His Difficulties

If you have a minute, please feel free to leave feedback/Amazon review of the book!

Muchas Gracias!

Made in the USA
Las Vegas, NV
01 June 2023

72801978R00073